A wild ride:

To Somewhere UnKnown

Forest Fyer

Published by endaStampa Press
Toronto, Ontario
Email: endapress@gmail.com

Book Design: Spence Clarke
Book Photographer: AJ Rosenberg, Photoberg Studios 2012
Book Interior: Jennie Clarke

First Edition
Canada, United Kingdom, USA

9 7 8 – 0 9 8 7 7 7 3 9 – 6 - 8

FIRST EDITION

~ Table of contents ~

the pages of this book contain words
and pictures collected for your enjoyment.
there are no page numbers as each piece
holds an individual place in line.

"The Shogun Garden"
contains select photos accompanied by
particular pieces scribed as companion
statements.

~ Introduction ~

If you are reading this then a hardy 'CHEERS' to us all as we have made it through the infamous 12-21-2012 portal.

The pages in this book contain a collection of adventures, perceptions, and conversations that took place on this *'Wild Ride To Somewhere Unknown'* leading up to what many hope to be an opening to a time of more consciousness and awareness of humankind and a larger connection of beings.

As one travels through life, all of the places you go as well as the people you meet are on journeys of their own. Our times cross paths with these other travelers forever connecting them through the positive and the negative of our interactions creating a powerful and undeniable network. With the history of mankind being dated back further and further as we grow wiser, this connecting network grows deeper and stronger allowing for a more open line to those times and events in our past that have made us the empowered beings we are.

This particular day as an example, 12-12-12 where an uncountable amount of people have interacted simultaneously at 12:12 am and 12:12 pm by some standard of time and adjusted to different zones.

It has been honored with many titles, World Hoop Day
World Meditation Day, Mic Check Day "mic check 1~2
1~2 1~2", all of which have lead to an ever growing
connection of positivity and interaction. The more
positive put into the network the more positive
the return is, and negative will come calling on its own.

Also this week is a chance to watch a great meteor
shower: the Geminids, so named because they appear to
shoot away from the constellation of Gemini.
This is a really reliable shower, generally putting out as
many as 100 meteors per hour! It peaks on the evening to
the morning of Dec. 13/14, but usually has a decent
showing for a couple of days before and after the peak.

Fortunate circumstances allowed me to be under the
journey tutelage of a Sage for some time. Among the
many 'lessons' I narrowed a short list of what has proven
most useful and somewhat rephrased them to a less
confusing language which I share with the reader here.

The choices you make determine the life you live,
and the worst mistake to make is a waste of talent.

If it haint got a point, don't mean yea gotta not do it.

Saucy is good especially on your demons.

Slutty princess are only worth a wooden nickel.

If the cards ain't face up walk away from the table.

Some day's you'll lead people into light, remember how
the light hurts your eyes when it first hits 'em, well it
hurts theirs to...now go get me a coke.

~To drink you

Taste the sip I seek
Sensing you wash, it fills me
In light of your presence

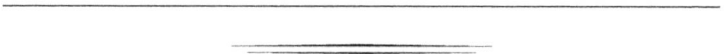

~To Taste you

Tangled tongues unwind
Imperfections, long lost life
Jubilant spirit rise

~To Breath You
Melodious scent
Caresses my foundation
Base to crest I vibe

~To Leave you

Don't you let me go
I did not stay for the stain
Licked flame, calls me home

~A stream of self awareness

As you step on my fate yet can't make me hate cause you know it's not in me.

My feet on the ground, i lean on a cloud and mountains are my step stool.

You point that disgrace at some other place cause im not the soul who damned you.

I live through life striding through strife paving a way for those who follow.

I cannot deny some parts inside have done went and died

but

that does not mean I do not love you.

I see down inside right through your third eye to the soul that is in you.

There is a chance to make yourself dance if the rhythm of love your tuned to,

and

you know it is fate that we all erase the hate that binds you.

So let it begin don't deny that grin and follow where truth will lead you.

Cause there is no doubt that life aint about using blame as the hand rail that guides you.

With this world that turns and the fires that burn, love and lights surrounds you.

Time will always cleans no matter what lens you decide to gaze through,

you know where to start if you listen to your heart and ignore those things that faked you.

~The Barker

Had a dog, his name was Jack--

put him in the barn and he peed thru a crack.

Had a dog, his name was Mike--

he knew a trick, he could ride a bike.

Had a dog, his name was Pete--

if you wiggled your toes he would lick your feet.

Had a dog, his name was Sammy--

he had good connections around S. Miami.

Come one come all, see 'Jo-Jo' the dog faced boy. He walks...he talks...he spits and he chews. With his amazing wife 'Sally Pinkwell' the bearded lady. All for one dime...one tenth of one dollar and you can feast your eyes on feats of ocular amazement...for an extra three cents adults can step thru the green curtain to take a swim with 'Lulu' as she pours her 'one and only in the whole of the world show'300+ lbs. of Erotic Delight, onto your platters of curiosity...step back son yer botherin me.

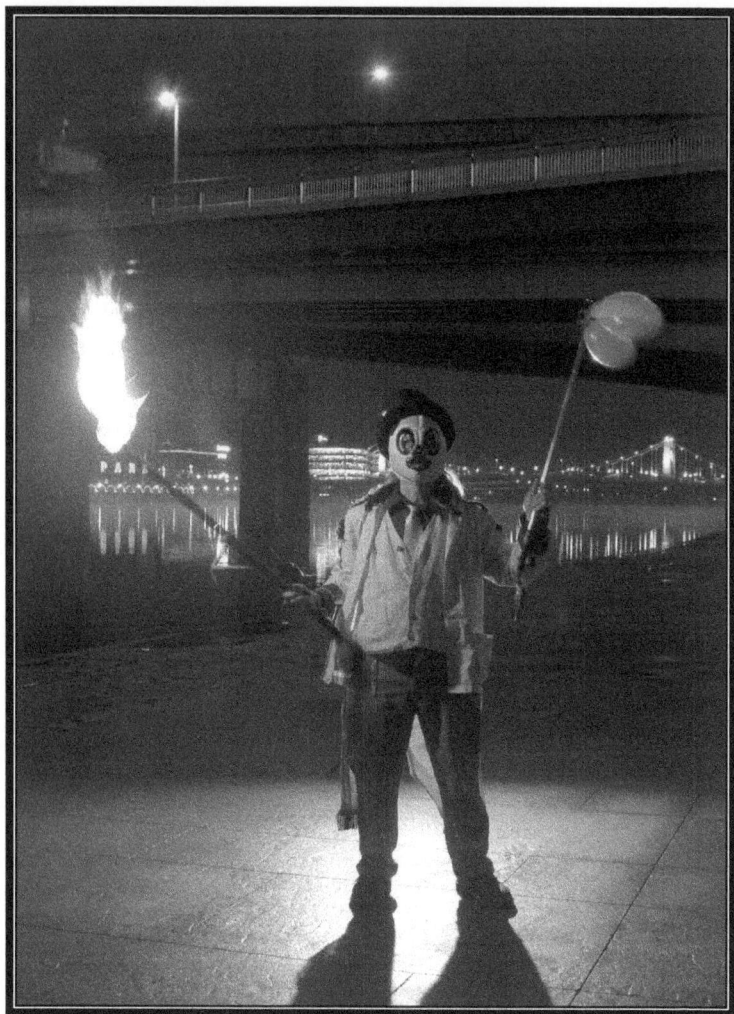

© Matthew Blake Photography
Shadows

not with an uncertain emotion or feeling but the utmost
of being he says it and with such guile and confidence,
he merely whispers it she knows that truth or not she
will believe him for the
eternity of shadow marks etched upon the floor.

~Sea of red...ocean of green

Snowflakes screaming senselessly
Sunshine sounds silently.

Veiling a time to be.

Miles meander meaninglessly,
Measuring morose movements.

Tapped into the rapture unfolding.

Black sack attack,
Fact lacked tact.

Come watch a clown dance.

Sublime time line,
Rhyme sign mine.

Turnstiles roll with the punches.

~As the sun edges

behind the large buckeye tree casting it's cooling late
afternoon shadow across the plaza. Morton and Jerald
are enjoying a well timed ice coffee amidst the parade
of hustle bustle. In regards to what you about to read
here, a conversation for consideration.

Morton-i have these 'things' and these 'things' and well...
they have 'stuff' on them. not necessarily so much stuff
that one would be concerned about something as trivial
a point as amount, but more along the lines of a
beguilingly vast 'how d id that stuff get there'
conundrum if you will. even with the precise scale
comparison of the what possibilities truly exist
as to the exact origin eagerly combined with endlessly
imagined confirmed identifications of said 'stuff' the
scales of lady justice tip profusely heavy
to the deciding yaw of 'how the hell did that get there'.

Jerald-The sooner you move through the acceptance stage, the sooner you can get that "stuff" off of your "things".

Just sittin there starin at it ain't doin nobody a licka good

Morton-well said good sir, but might it be in the vast knowledge you obviously have on the situation the solution of 'how' one is to go about removing 'stuff' from their 'things' if they are still vexed by the 'how did it get there' aspect...hmmm?

Jerald- Perhaps you should talk to a "specialist." But they will probably tell you the same thing, and charge you twice as much.

Morton- Completely smashing statement, for what you have done good 'sir' is pleasantly present perplexing principals surrounding the subject matter on not necessarily the concept of what could be called an 'expert' on any matter, that is obviously a procured document from some manner of governing body of 'experts' but now the query is what does one study to become a said 'expert' on the 'removal' of 'stuff' who's indigenous origins or molecular make up is not the consideration but an 'expert' on the 'removal' of 'stuff' with a cocooned concept of 'how' said 'stuff' arrives at any given station. i must ponder this now...are there any radish's left?

~ Wanders in rue

Step through the portal that knows no bounds--
holding my hand
See the light with no determinable source--
holding my hand
Bend your ear listening to majikal sounds--
holding my hand
Open your heart with no recourse--
holding my hand
Dance on the ground as a beautiful stage --
holding my hand
Warm your skin from heat of the sun--
holding my hand
View every day as a blank page--
holding my hand

Stay with me 'til a better one--
holding
my
hand

~ Vintage lust

Coming back up down from then,

 what once was anyway, not really sure?

Only because doing the once or twice before

afforded no cure.

Calling back the quick, a twitty crime?

Who offers the frame, not mine.

Could you be the one that time has left lost?

Protective soul shield at little to no cost.

~ Mr. Chibbitts kiss

Mad Wild Beautiful Thang,

Alluring kitten-dangerous fang.

Manipulated ink from needle tips, eternally

blessed by succulent lips.

Valiant knight neck guarded,

truth full souls never parted.

Beaming light into dark niches,

get busy livin you mother bitches.

~Morton and Jerald, swimming.

Throughout forever Morton and Jerald were all ways quite the pair. Whenever one was, the other were as well. As on this wonderful autumn day, hills a brim with brilliant color and faint wisps of winters breath in the spicy air.

We find Jerald swimming alone in the deep warm blue waters off an island in the south pacific, somewhere. Doing the breast stroke with vigor from a long planned well deserved vacation.

Carrying that smile born from one thousand pub laughs, beating heart filled with effervescent joy from Morton's last proclamation as he tossed off his mortal coil to Davey Jones's locker.

The word's shouted as both body's ripped through the air by the force of their rental boat exploding "At least my right eye will quit hurting!" would eternally echo in his ears.

~ Screaming in the tub

Echoes left on bathroom tile,
Palatial feelings undetermined.

Wearing concrete eyelid
night vision goggles to seaway
the rolling lights that lead in all directions home.

Narrowly avoiding the complex set of undivided
grooves criss crossed in a juxt2pose manner of speaking
from ones other face.

At a visioned mind titans request all became lost,
in a manner of speaking,
calling for that which has no name
and should not be spoken of.

Great light speaking in tongues,
Crumpled news litter
Box treasures
Alive,
With misleads
Challenging ur cause
Maybe Shiva does dance right

~As

misty
fogs
blanket
unknown
sunrises
pliable
parameters
pushed
engorging
structural
integrity
upheld
longingly
discrete
emotions
melt
frozen
guide
walls
announcements

~ Lost under the one

A vast lonely chill that will not sleep off, led by the
surreal rhythmic chimes of a post-modern belly dancer,
riding mesmeric aromas haunting the
hungered.

Lips bleating hollowed calls lost in the night,
silhouettes cast windows frost life box glowing
inside.

Lead me to the dream, silk swaddled sweet passion
extreme, rewards for the 'lucky' who drew that line in
the sands?

Reaching with every repetitive hum that passes,
for the horizon, for the ground.

For the stars reaching to warm the
'vast lonely chill that will not sleep off.'
maybe next time'round…maybe.

~ Folded papers

Tell the tales of heart songs, plucked by the fingers of an earth bound angels hand

Dauntlessly carry tiding scabs of over picked wounds

Lost promises of earthly delight

Knowledge kept knowing

Ways of the soul to travel forthwith, in a direction not previously perceived

Copy data reporting intelligent informational word story's

...should be unfolded

~ Burro wall

Class fought reins,

lifelong drains

blowing ashes from the matters.

Monsters trock marily through the dark night

Casting devilish stares

at those who dare pop their flaming

bubbles with green fire,

naughty castling's who shite

from three feet in the air,

go got grown of hearded giggles

thrown their mix of a bunch

to the sand box of nightchilde.

Trunk dug cave walls sparkle

as a broken glass bed for expended shells.

Quacks leading the blind

on faster shortcuts to longer routes

all--hell bent for leather...blood.

Climb in the box

that rocks with no top

and send the colors sailin.

Gaspin eyes

did wonder at the site

unbeheld

and

away the things that never were

shoulda been,

came to be.

Ghetto superstar,

way to fucking far--not knowing who you are.

Peace be with those children

who have come

and

gone to play,

may I never grow so tall

as to not see the sparkle of wonder in their eyes--as those

who lead have taught

example is the plan,

and

welcome that which is coming.

Rejoice the splenderious unknown

© Matthew Blake Photography

~ Postal Seasonings

Cause yourself, treat to sweet

        Buy the atone, bitter and creep.

Cobalt blue, save the day

        Shredded life, swings to a frey.

Peddled varmints, lost to cause

        Befuttled mutt, insights too pause.

~Do Not Walk

Burn for the minute...
burn for the day,
Burn to walk...
Burn to play!
Burn with fingers...
Burn with toes,
Burn, who measures...
Burn, who knows?
Burn pure a purpose,
easy to see
Burn pure a purpose,
sure to please.
Burn away the darkness lies and greed.
Burn away to enlighten truth's generosity.
Burn their world shall see
Burn there love will be.
Burn at dawn
Burn at night
Burn into life
Burn...outta sight.

~Door Knob Signs

When the hand is raised
Do Not Disturb us inside
Unless you have food

~ The Edgers

forced to the fringes, riders of the edge, the ones
responsible for keeping a moving cycle to things.
regulators of expansion and pushers of the per norm.
swinging bubbles of reality with no obvious reasoning.
the ticket check in bastards. the creators of
the snicker the point and the guffaw. the ones who cheat
death by living life. providers of the taste. the ones who
cause a stir and break molds. the mavericks of life. the
path makers and conscious shakers that grab bulls by
their horns and wrestle em frontier style. the wide eyed
exciters with a razor sharp distant gaze calibrated with
an oddly curios perspective crowned with a broadened
beaming brow. easily recognized and hard
to forget, fortunes encased in every chance encounter
and the tales they tell with each step taken. gather the
surreal the crazy misguided and slightly different
chew them up like the tasty sweet gum balls of life we
are, blow a radiant bubble for the world to see...then
POP! It.

©Karmiclsle

~ U 4 E A

Felt
around
stumble upon,
crumble
dipt.

Puff
cheese
enthusiastic,
lessons
grit.
burn
critical
disengage,
quiver
spit.

Boss
explode
playanation,
undress
whip.
Done over hipitty blot,
demon masks swim in froth...lost

~ Embers in fyer, man

Preceded darkness enters into the ceaseless crucible crux
glowing in lighten mint. Charred shadows breath creeps
with willful stares at dissolving footprints sweetened by
juice drops cascading from the fresh ripped vine...big
leaves baoding their rhyme.

 Swung by the worlds own tail--rising door chime,
sevens forth nine--directed gusts in the petticoat sail.

Frolic pyre mad dance across the pallet stacked fields--
bursting balloons, flashy fumes, taped nipple flame
eating baboons...leading a Charleston with shiny chains
set to the sight, suspended, warily watching, gash goes
the night.

 Stamped approval on that which is done--nomads wake
a polished sheen, proper attire donned, slick back the
grease pack--stand asta one.

~ Faces In Places

the ones who survived saw the predators faces...
the ones who survived saw the predators faces,
in the trees in the shrubs where ever they roam,
they saw the shapes and the faces, then got gone.
sometimes see shapes in the oddest of places,
sometimes see faces that aren't even faces.
they saw the faces, the ones who evolved.

~ Find You Face

Look around you now
See who is your crowd
In the metroid life of shit
Comfort abounds this fellowship
FOR HERE!
Thoughts are spoken
visions bear seed
a shell you may carry, however
inside we shall see.

From way back before when the carousel went round
joyful spirits have had
final say upon this hallowed ground.

Movers and Shakers
Hustlers and Fakers
Givers and Takers
Mystics and Makers
Hell we have even had the ever popular self proclaimed
martyr or two.

From the telegraph of the trees
to the crystals you stand on now:
Withered smiles to Happy frowns
Unbridled glee to Manipulated downs
Tattered patchwork to Wedding Gowns
Smoke house smells to Dank clowns

Anything you need to Pizza you cant turn down
We have all seen the sound.
With each and every turn this way and that,
those who you follow like who follow you do,
some wear the same hat.

And we all know the feeling 'Hey, what's the deal here?'
with a conversation that's all too familiar.
"sorry bro, I'm on a mission that's gonna be great,
gotta hustle to get there it's close to eight."
"don't worry man it's only half past nine
we all run on Quarry Time"

We have had kinfolk here, brothers and sisters, who
tossed their mortal coils sometime in the past.
Let's give us a moment to remember what is we had,
shared loves sorrows and laughs.
after a moment of silence {....................} we all yell,
'IT WAS A BLAST'

And when we all leave here take what is inside
Remember how close we all are
we share the same sky.

~Fire toy Safety
First set it ablaze
Second figure how to play
Next is safety third

~ Homage to Green Eyes

Green Eyes is the brother of Blue Eyes a pair of siblings who walk of the earth, sometimes called transient. In the lines that follow will be the tale of what is the standard setter of bad days for me when i heard it, and for some a shocking tale.

Late afternoon on a typically sweltering hot late July day. sitting on the patio steps of an ultra
retro hip cafe nestled on the fringes to the bustling downtown of a big city trying to fend off the swirl of garbled fluff conversed around me and I notice the consistent bobbing stride of Green Eyes hurrying up the walk. Once he recognized me sitting where we had chatted a few times before he stopped and asked for smoke. As I handed it to him I noticed that he was overly roughed up, Green Eyes was known for gettin into some shit now and again, but this was that kind of 'what the hell happened' look.

'So I decided I would call it an early night', shoulda known better i said, he laughed and continued 'so I went ahead and got up under the bridge and just when I got comfy outta no where comes five frat lookin boys and I could tell they wanted nothin but trouble.

So I figger I'd try and slip out real quick but they caught me and with five of 'em I couldn't hold my own. After they got me down and had me kicked pretty good they took my plasma sellin money went through my back pack then drug me up by their house where they beat on me some more while waitin on the cops to show up. What they had told the cops was that they caught me tryin to break in and got a little carried away stoppin me, of course piggy don't care it's just another street bum got beat up one way or another, so I get the ride down town.

After questioning they decided to let me go, at two o'clock in the mornin. Now I'm walkin from way the other side of down town been awake for almost twenty four hours and had the shit kicked outta me.
I see a trash truck empty a dumpster and figured I could get a few hour nap so I climbed on in and got laid out.

Well sometime after I had fall asleep I got woke up cause the routes was messed up or somethin and another truck had showed up and was dumpin the one I was in.

Now itsa good thing I already been on that ride a couple times before so I just slid out on the dump into the back of the truck and start makin my way to the little hatch door, which it's a good thing cause it started packin up. I got the door pushed open and was about half wiggled out when the driver noticed me and took to beatin on me with a tire buddy or sumthin while he was on the radio callin dispatch who was sending the cops, again. Of course the cops show up, and of course they aint to worried bout another street bum that got beat up, and again I get the ride down town. While the questionin was goin on a couple of the officers from earlier recognized me and I was released, again. Now I'm tryin to finally walk back up to the bridge an see if I can find my brother.'

And after a hardy 'thanks friend' Green Eyes strode away. In the roughly five or so minutes that he told me his tale not only did he set the bar example for bad days to come for me, but a standard by which to handle them.

~ Hope

one more look into your eye,
one extra chance to breath your sigh.
one greater time to dance in the rain,
one further opportunity to be insane.
another time will come

~ maximus

step lively gone away, yet to be another day.
sunlight mocking every move, nighttime stockings--
flamming shrooms.
cast along smitley, functioned blightly, packed in tightly-
-feel the day?
Trashcan confessionals, shit house lawyers, lambic ho's...
grotesquely iridescent display mongrels barking
haphazard spirals characteristicly unbequethed
heretofore.
lead by archaic dinoliptic riders, purveyors remented in
their quest of foreloinment.
Why am I not surprised.

~ Glow Love

Born on the free-way half where's between Salt Rock and Radnor, subsequently raised on a mayonaise farm by a pack of wild beatnecks.

At the early age of nine our hero was run over by a back-hoe, sparks commenced and his face caught fire.
acting in haste a very brave beatneck put the fire out with a rake, and a hardy expulsion of liquid human waste.

At the age of thirteen our hero was shipped to a freak community on the outskirts of the Orange Blossom Trail, a well known party strip extending through the greater Orlando area, for training.

Being assigned to two general posts, the first being towl man for Cinnamon. she was a Go-Go club dancer who's main act consisted of placing three colored ping-pong balls, red yellow and green, into her femen in opening and then ejecting them one at a time towards a brandy snifter on the bar. the patrons place pool bets on which if any of the colored balls made it into the snifter.

and through personal conversation our hero found out that Cinnamon could at will make which or however many she chose.

The second post assigned to our hero was that of gem handler for Diamond, another Go-Go club worker with an exceptional talent which consisted of an act where the patrons, for a nominal fee of course, put their name in a fish bowl.

and the lucky name drawn out was permitted to place the gem, an ordinary egg, into her feminine opening.

she would then perform a personal lap dance. Upon completion of this dance if the gem was not at least soft boiled the lucky recipient got half of the money in the fish bowl.

if it was hard boiled all he got was the gem
and one Not long thereafter our hero decided to join a band of gypsie elephant maters, mule skinners and snake oil salesmen. helluva good lap dance.

Being assigned as the official snake squeezer and mop man for the elephant department was not what made him leave so abruptly but the discovery an underground 'glow-love' operation. Glow-Love being the delicate combination of glowstick liquid sex lube and just the right touch of vapo rub for tingle.

the niche market being dance clubs and ware house parties or any where sweaty half naked crowds of girating people could be found.

not that the venture was unfruitful but the glowstick supplier caught on to the high profit end and using his own connections began to choke out any competition with lower prices.

Not at all in a desperate move our hero decides that using his biker gang experience to muscle in on some counterfeit French toast scam would prove to be not worth the effort and he takes on the position of caravan guardian for a giant waffle front.

The company actually sold small boxes without paying any tarriff on them, they did this by hiding what they were actually doing with a waffle store front, and our heroes position in all this was the official counterjockey.

Guarding the caravans was easier if they designated an official position for him, and the promise of future growth was encouraging.

However, the gypsies had found out about the waffle store front and muscled in thereby eliminating any possible growth potential.

So to kill some time and generally feel better about himself he decided to be a herder at the local chicken farm.

Daunted by a lack of challenge this parlayed into what most free americans would refer to as a bunch of dumb stuff, turning himself into a 50' human sparkler and dancing the whirly gig with burning suns attached to silver chains.

Very scary but it allows for some serious me time, and a well protected personal space.

The problem being that doing this act in the mall while naked brought about repercussions both physical and legal allowing for well...more me time.

cheatin ass paperclips and stretched rubberband balls aside,
the hero in us must keep trying or they really are not our hero's
now are they?
and as a liver of life do not fall prey to definitions that you do not comprehend

~ Mortar

Nails grind into my love,
with the ratta-tat-tat of a live machine gun.
Taste our passions morbid sweet,
feel me kiss you bullet deep.
Set the site on my silhouetted figure,
clear you mind then pull the trigger.
Tear me open see the blood,
white hot soul makes you numb.
Scream and fight if you care,
eye see the toll standing there

~ My Time

My time in the woods, i think back...
coffee taste best from an acorn cap.
My time in the city, i think back...
soul needs to taste a little gritty, place for that.
My time inside me, i think back...
love life's joyous journey, blood stain fact.
My time where i go, i think back...
My time where i go, exactly that.

~ Tore

Reading the words
as
they are spoken
from lust swelled lips,
ruby taste of opiates
cling to the breath
of hundred year
dead poets words,
fire burning inside.

Heavens world
set free on earth
through grace
 from plastic sheer latex
the guile will
of
the cantankerous rhythm.

Mortal coils
perform the dance of a diabolo,
whispered winds
whirled fairy wings keep time.
Diagrams printed by the ancients followed,
sources unresolved--matter left behind.

Spices envied by the finest ham,
long comes the tail
of star speckled paths

leading to†maypole glee.

Lines abound,
distant harbour
hues highlight horizons,
flight bears witness
to a bold jump.

Step through the portal that knows no bounds--
holding my hand
See the light with no determinable source--
holding my hand
Bend your ear listening to majikal sounds--
holding my hand
Open your heart with no recourse--
holding my hand
Dance on the ground as a beautiful stage --
holding my hand
Warm your skin from heat of the sun--
holding my hand
View every day as a blank page--
holding my hand

Stay with me 'til a better one--
holding
my
hand

~ Terra

Light reflective ink needled in skin,
is that where life begins?
Earth walking aboard rainbow coloured swirling
twirling space rock,
dancing with the pulse.
Show us your dance fairmaid.
Dance with fevered joy passionate purpose
manipulated burning white hot suns
join your raptures bliss,
their petite exquisiteness personified
by mad orbits of the terra,
casting their glow divinely.
Misty cool lake of light
swims above your head
as the night begins its sleep,
shrouded in faint wisps lurching
from eves companion

"Take rest night child's playground"
purveyor of all things
reverently healed
by your slumber,
ray will lead adventures way in search for that
which you aboundly provide.

Speckled spots spring forth.

Purged colours express a jig through stratus

suspended sponges.

Ancient fingers creep,

encroaching fear upon the hearts of the mundane.

"Heed ye warned,"
Sally ahead
finding brave of heart
true of soul,
dare to say
a liver of life.

bring us that
which you nurture so well.

~New Moon Haiku

Bringer of the tide
Taste you feel you relight me
Gift giving ally

©Matthew Blake Photography
Fire Toys

~Fire toy Safety

First set it ablaze

Second figure how to play

Next is safety third

~ Tyme

Once when the start came,

limpid pools and stars shined.

Death was nothing more than dad in a box,

much like a bee sting on the hand...it healed, never.

moon rose tide ebbed,

ever shadowed in the light.

heart felt strains evermore, dirty hair

clean air,

forgotten lies untold

sunshine smitten kitten felt the warmth from a yard or

two.

begin again with the night lings

cast orange hued shadows, deceivers of all

believers of none.

truth be told 'ozone level cranial locations lead to

downfalls'

hard ones at that.

read the scars as their tales are told,

unbegun at the beginning and

never done at the end.

life giving woosh, heat feels right leading,

following from the front.

time, my brothers,

is ever present in the here and now

that which has never will be

and

 that which will be is not current.

where to point that firearm

weapon if you choose not to be chosen,

empty the wading pool of adventure,

envelope the depths.

©Matthew Blake Photography

~ Observing passages

Doorways vary from place to place. And in my travels
I have made special effort taking detailed metal note
of these mighty vessels for passage. There are those
special made to swing wide, and some have never really
closed the way it should.

monstrous entrances bearing roost to enchantingly
ominous beasts with a single purpose of creation for
knocking.

Chiseled tributes of flora fauna and heroes of man stand
unyielding guard against any doubt the amazing
wonders abounding on the other side.

I have frequented doors that are mostly glass, made me
wonder why some doors are there and you cannot see
thru them at all, no matter how hard you try.

Some doors are kept dusted and painted purty, and i
have barely made it thru some that are kicked slammed
and sound like a hurdy-gurdy.

Green doors brown ones wood steel plated metal custom cut 'double hung' impressive.

So I imagine people and picture a door, and wonder 'what door for them?'

What manner of portal guard would this people design as their perfect door.

Ones with special handles hidden pass codes and no particular discerning mode of operation.

Ones with welcome mats woven of eco friendly design with a smart match color trim, a hipster door if you will.

And I find from the deepest of delving within myself on this matter, imagining archways of this and that

I wonder which, door is for me?

~ when rain stops in time

time stops for an instant in life, with more to come.
counting the bricks the steps the drips, with more to
come.
reading words in the haze the gaze they say, with more
to come.
that chair that box that door that table, with more to
come.
jumping falling scratching crawling, with more to come.
grabbing stars from the sky, with more to come

~ The Song Bird Blues

With the degree of warmth steadily dropping from what
was a low digit anyway, our little friend the si-si bird
was certain that he was not long for this world.

But as fortune did happen si-si's way, 'Hoss' the
barnyard bull happened to plop directly upon him.

 Now Hoss, he was a damn fine plopper from way back
and lay upon si-si about as fine a patty as a freezin cold
bird could ask for.

After a very short time si-si's degree of warmth began to
rise, so he became quite enthused at the thought
of survival.

This made for a very happy si-si bird, so he began to do
what happy little birds do oh so well, which is
lift his beak to the sky and began to sing his si-si bird
song.

Some creatures take great comfort in hearing a si-si bird
song while some creatures are unsurpassingly annoyed
by its ill timed execution.

And yet to others such as 'Pete' the barnyard cat, it was an indication of potential food for her and her kittens.

Answering to her natural instict, she sought out the source swiftly removed the si-si bird and slay her pray. taking it back to shelter as a meal for her brood.

Pundit expressions:
Some say this old story is to show that you can sometimes tell the future just not exactly how it will go. Yet a few, of which i myself can be included, believe the true morale to this fable is that just because someone shits on you that does not make them your enemyand whoever digs you out aint always your friend...howboutchyea.

~ Silliest Of Strings

Strings that string and strings that play...the strings on a
heart fray.

Fray the twine that ties a knot...know that love is not
forgot.

Love that is heavy weight of a feather...love souls all
ways together.

Souls that bear fruit save the day, souls without
truth...them, I slay.

~ Spinning the white heat

I see you standing, star scarred hands wringing fear
from
your soul. forming half frozen puddles around all but
discarded feet.

A glint of refuge curtains muddled truth beyond
perception.

Grotesque glamor woven cloak shields a fractured heart
from the wispy fingered frigid swirl emanating around
you.

I see you
Molten tears from obvious disconcerted
joy, complimenting a trusty swig on a summer night.
Frosty cold smile blazing within the hearth, pleading the
weigh for viciously nurturing anchors sediment within.

I see you
vinyl throne beckoning the lost warmth of previous
purveyors producing jargon bringing again the mislaid
joys of promised lies
forgotten truths and wilted loves.
Buffed old change kept from fresh inexact not new starts
nurture a wantin beasts belly empowering it's depletion,
hungered hallowed hunted.

I see you
Adorning a wistful gaze upon mysteries abound, the
sights sounds smells of disoriented
passions fiercely tantalize.
Endlessly overflowing tide pool waves exploding love
desire hunger from its vicious path, as you dance to the
distant crack of discord. It shoves it's gift of death and
tattered hubcaps into holes of reality, paying tolls with
abused stockings and wine goblet ashtrays gracefully
balanced among tenseless body parts curling the smokey
haze that defts from whispered desires. While doors
creak with a sense of accomplishment.

I see you
When you reach out that wicked hand confident in some
manner of plan...I stand, to take the needled grasp deep
into calloused abyss reaches of my illuminated soul.
Unyielding tentacles ensnare putrid offending limbs
drawing them ever closer upon my chalice of life, muscle
bone blood heart forged weapon of truth endeavors to
persevere for life, I see you.

~ Them

A quick note my brothers and sisters on the subject matter of 'them'or 'they' as sometimes referred to.

The 'they' have the distinction of being 'them' thus making 'them' not 'us', and of course 'we' are not the 'they' either.

Giving 'us' full right of power to be the 'we' 'we' choose and the 'them' 'they' would like to be, whatever that is.

So long as 'we' stay over here with 'us' and 'they' stay over there with 'them' all will be fine. 'We' have had reports of some minor mixings of 'us' with 'them' out on our furthest borders to the south as well as confirmed sightings where 'they' ventured into where 'we' are to the west.

Please take extreme precaution if any of 'us' interact with 'them' and furthermore, incidents where 'they' end up where 'we' are, please act accordingly.

Thank you, and as all ways 'we' enjoy being 'us'

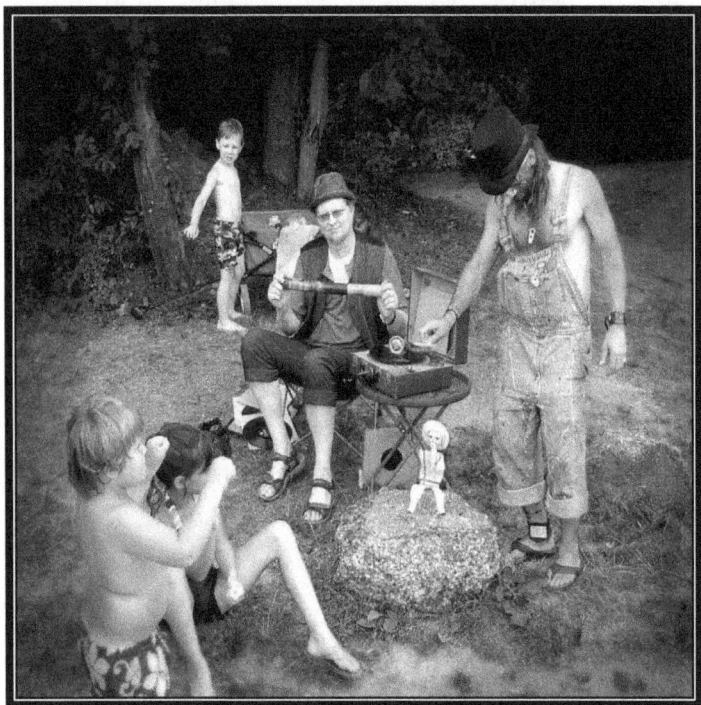

© Sue A. Wasconis

~ moments

distance effort intent purity love

forgiveness future

can all be decided in one glorious or shabby moment

my brothers and sisters,

enjoy them id get to riding.

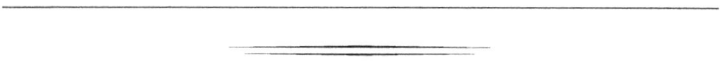

~ A tale of two birds

Five little horseies went trot, trot, trot

Five little horsies went plop, plop, plop

Five little toesies soon needed hoseies

Cause breathin through shit is tough.

~Up

down, left, right...
echoed screams guide the night.

grits, home fries, sliced tomatoes...
define the morning helloes.

tattered soul, clean shirt...
wretched bandage for a soul that's burnt.

leaving winter woes...
canvas shoes home for toes.

laughing, crying, dying...
the tickets paid get to riding.

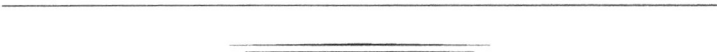

~ An Ode To Waffle House

Strain the times of past through glorious batter,
scatter me smother me cap me, reward me my birth.

Suckling of the bacon beasts hide, our lives
forever entwine.

The light you cast is a comforting glow on the horizon
beckoning to me.

Inciting my heart to palpitate through its lead walled
prison, choking tears from my eyes.

Tongue swollen from apathy I breath the familiar air.
Enraptured by the thrill again...I reach, to be.

~ Bacon

sizzling sounds sing
how your aroma delights
any meal you tweak.

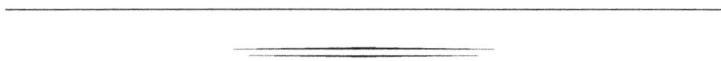

~ Fyer

there is certainly a passion when it comes to
matters of the creature known as fire. it is
a physical entity that is created exists and dissipates.
if one manages to survive thrill riding along the thin
edge of a controlled accident that allows for the
beautiful symbiotic inception of a vision which
sometimes for no more than a brief moment unlocks
a primal connection in humanity, then a very pure
connection between humanity and art is created. when
man's comprehension of how to appropriate a working
relationship with this fickle elemental was established
the capacity to expand the borders of his existence to the
limits of his own will became possible. it is true nature
within the duality of man to reach back that far in his
past and bring forth a tangable connection in an artistic
expression as a tribute to the will and power that makes
us who and what we are
as humans

~ Acknowledgement ~

~ Beth Blue, if not for one of her many selfless efforts this writer is convinced he would be in an unimaginable place.

~ Muse xo

To the energies I have come across that have taught me and I them, it's our job to keep things rolling even if we do not have a plan.

And to the Eskimo I hung out with around Key West FLA in '93 that convinced me to use my natural talent to earn us beer and pizza money I thank you for starting an avalanche brother.

Cover Photography ©AJ Rosenberg, Photoberg Studios 2012

~ John 'Pops' Dickerso

i kill darkness and ignorance!

With deep roots in Mu Shan and Taekwondo martial arts combined with an addiction to adrenaline, expression in the fire arts was inevitable. Using skills honed as a street performer, the since birth desire to entertain has evolved into an all sense enhancing display of revelry adjustable for most any occasion.

The current apex of that adjustability is on display for you now. Tangled thoughts, whispered fears and, yes, the ever present knowledge that 'as i walk, i see beauty' has culminated from living for years under the guise of college advisory and the assistance of the Balkan Alliance International or BA-I, an international collection of expressionists from multiple levels of influence serving each other as a Hessian crucible.